KINDER KOLLEGE

Primary Copybook

Handwriting

Pre-K and Kindergarten

L. M. Logan
Patrice Juah
Ophelia S. Lewis

Village Tales Publishing
MINNEAPOLIS, MN

Copyright © 2020 by Liberia Literary Society

All rights reserved. No part of this publication may be reproduced, distributed or transmitted in any form or by any means, without prior written permission.

Village Tales Publishing
www.villagetalespublishing.com
www.oass.villagetalespublishing.com
www.villagetalespublishing.com/childrensbooks

Book Cover and formatting by OASS

ISBN: 9781942408557
LCCN: 2020905188

A Liberia Literary Society Educational Project

Printed in the USA

This book belongs to:
_____

How to care for your copybook.

1. Write with clean hands.
2. Turn pages carefully.
3. Keep your copybook in your bookbag when you're not using it.
4. Keep your copybook away from food and drinks.
5. Keep your copybook away from younger siblings and pets.
6. Only draw, write, and color where instructed to.

The first thing I do is always the same,
I pick up my pencil and write my name.

  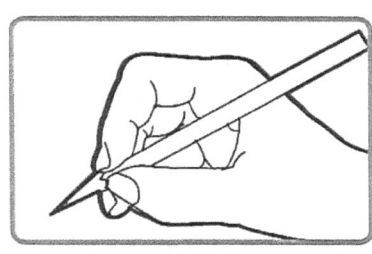

Sit down and place book flat in front of you.

Use your helper hand to hold the paper down while writing.

Correctly hold your pencil; only move the fingers when writing.

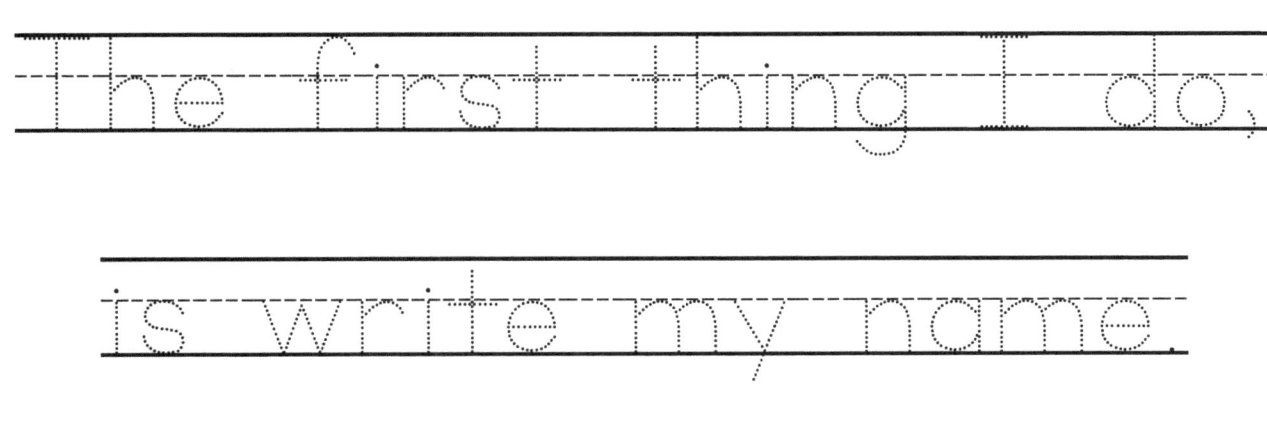

Contents

My Best Writing 103
Fix it Up 132
Where is it? 135
What is it? 137
Find The Missing Vowel Sound 139
My Favorite Animals 141
My Favorite Foods 143
Number Words 145
Who are They? 146
Which Group Do They Belong In? 148
My Favorite Words 150
Read, Trace, and Write The Words 151
Synonym Words 154
Compound Words 158
Rhyming Words 161
Read and Color 166
What Are They Doing? 168
I Know Opposite Words 170
Bible Lessons 172
Telling The Truth 180
Honesty 182
Friendship 184
Positive vs. Negative Behavior 186
Behavior Sort 188
Be a Buddy, NOT a Bully 189
Away With Bullying! 190
Sad, Mad, or Glad 192
Table Manners 194
My Best Art 195

Aa Bb Cc Dd
Ee Ff Gg Hh
Ii Jj Kk Ll
Mm Nn Oo Pp
Qq Rr Ss Tt
Uu Vv Ww Xx
Yy Zz

Name _____ Date _____

Name _____ **Date** _____

Name _____ **Date** _____

Name _____ **Date** _____

Name _____ **Date** _____

Name _____ **Date** _____

Name: Date:

Name: Date:

Name: Date:

Name: Date:

Name: Date:

Name: Date:

Name: Date:

Name: Date:

Name: Date:

Name: Date:

Name _____ **Date** _____

Name _____ Date _____

Name _____ Date _____

Name _____ **Date** _____

Name _____ **Date** _____

Name _____ Date _____

Name: Date:

Name: Date:

Name: Date:

Name: Date:

Name: Date:

Name: Date:

Name: Date:

Name: Date:

Name: Date:

Name: Date:

Name _____ **Date** _____

Name _____ Date _____

Name _____ **Date** _____

Name _____ **Date** _____

Name _____ **Date** _____

Name: Date:

Name: Date:

Name: Date:

Date:

Greeting:

Body:

Closing:

Signature:

Date:

Greeting:

Body:

Closing:

Signature:

Date:

Greeting:

Body:

Closing:

Signature:

Date:

Greeting:

Body:

Closing:

Signature:

Name: Date:

Name: Date:

Name: Date:

Name: Date:

Name: Date:

Name _____ Date _____

Name _____ Date _____

Name _____ **Date** _____

Name _____ **Date** _____

Name _____ Date _____

My Best Writing

My best writing

Letter

Trace. Write. Color the pictures that start with A.

104

Trace. Write. Color the pictures that start with C.

106

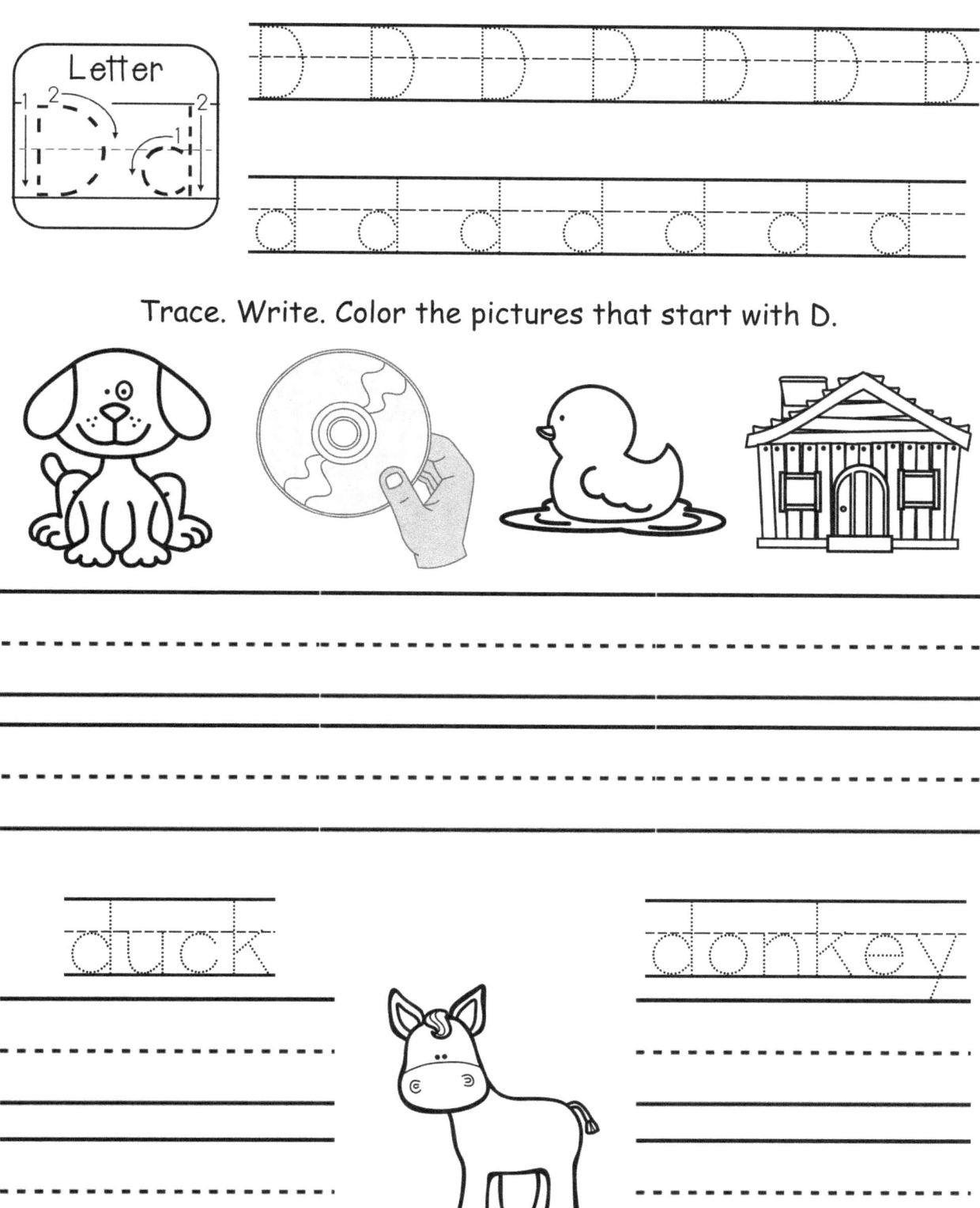

Trace. Write. Color the pictures that start with E.

Trace. Write. Color the pictures that start with G.

Trace. Write. Color the pictures that start with I.

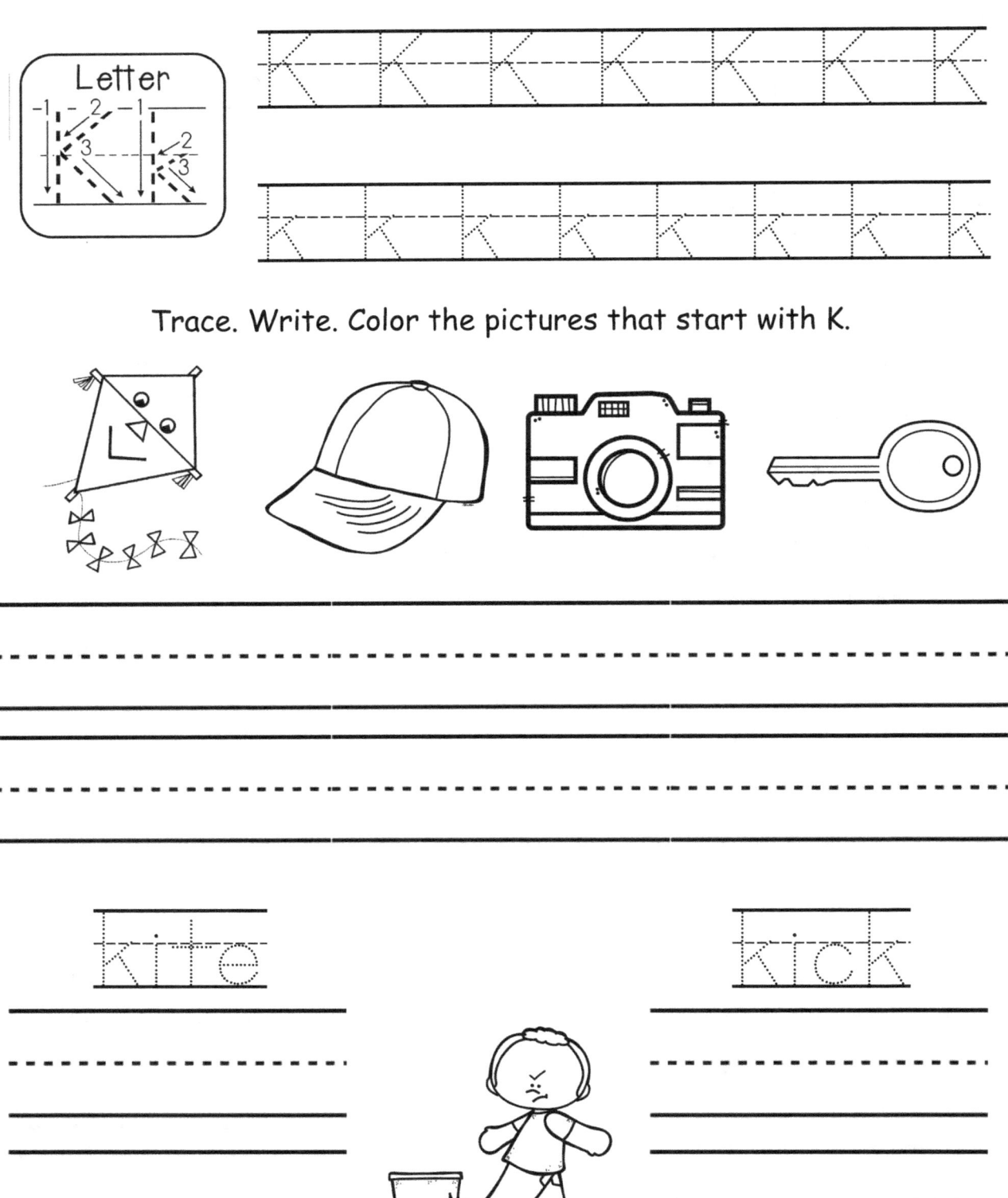

Trace. Write. Color the pictures that start with K.

114

Trace. Write. Color the pictures that start with M.

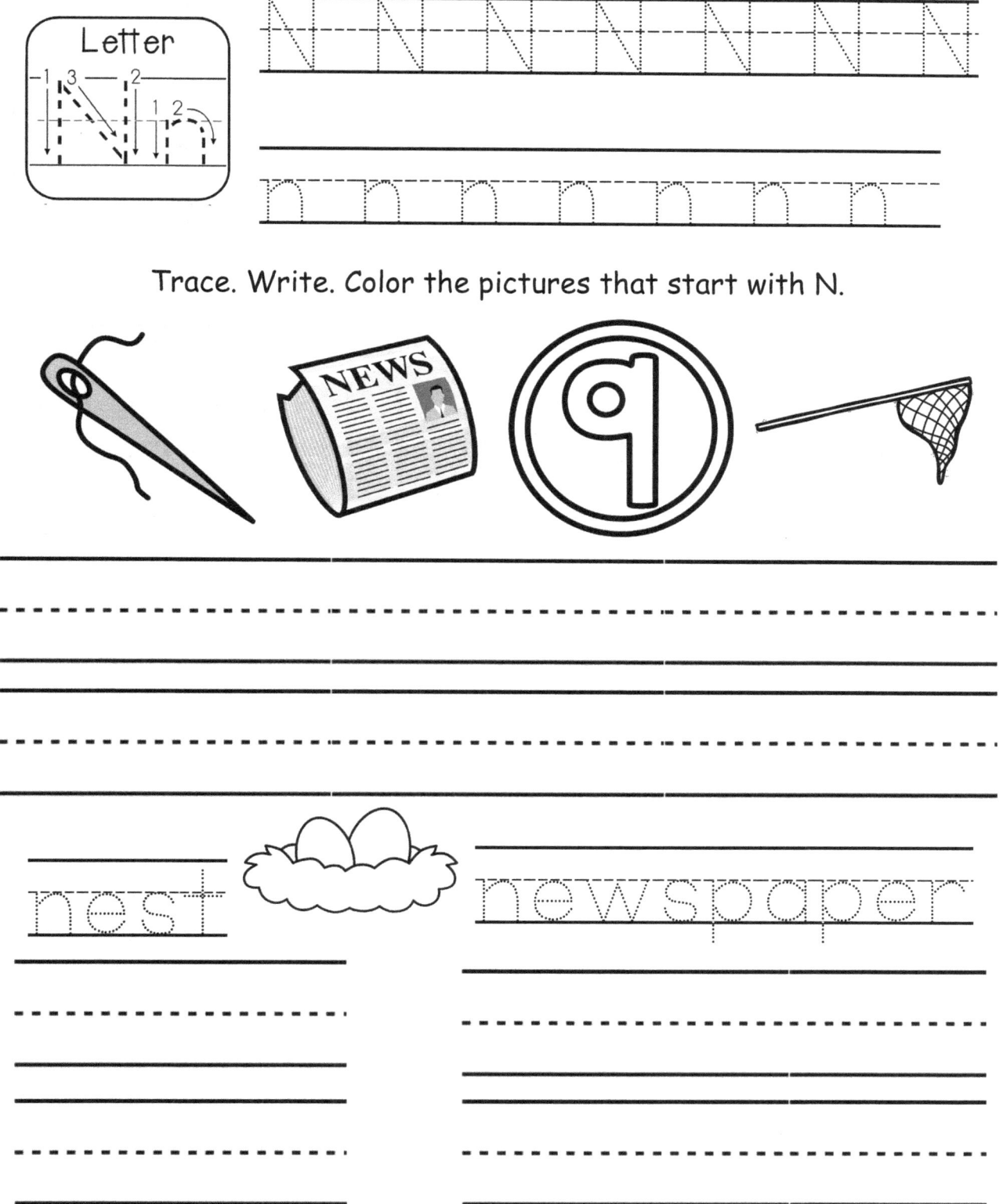

Trace. Write. Color the pictures that start with P.

Trace. Write. Color the pictures that start with R.

road

rock

Trace. Write. Color the pictures that start with T.

Trace. Write. Color the pictures that start with V.

Trace. Write. Color the pictures that start with W.

Trace. Write. Color the pictures that start with X.

xylophone   xray

127

Trace. Write. Color the pictures that start with Y.

Trace. Write. Color the pictures that start with Z.

Trace then write.

I am a writer.

I write with a purpose.

inform express argue

persuade explain

entertain   evaluate

WRITING

Let's write

131

Fix it Up

Don't forget to use CAPITALS, spaces, and an ending punctuation!

Question marks

Exclamation marks start at the top.

Periods touch the writing line.

canihavesome

Trace

Can I have some?

Write

Don't forget to use CAPITALS, spaces, and an ending punctuation!

hellomrbai

Trace

Hello Mr. Bai

Write

ilovejollofrice

Trace

I love jollof rice.

Write

whereismysock

Trace

Where is my sock?

Write

Don't forget to use CAPITALS, spaces, and an ending punctuation!

thisismyfavorite

Trace

This is my favorite!

Write

howdoyouspellit

Trace

How do you spell it?

Write

pleaseusesoap

Trace

Please use soap.

Write

Where is it?

Answer with full sentences.

bird	in	mud
boy	in	table
pig	on	bike
	on	cage

The pig is in the mud.

The ___ is ___ the ___.

The ___

Where is it?
Answer with full sentences.

ant	in	basket
ball	in	table
dog	on	bike
pig	on	wagon

What is it?

It is a _____

It is a

What is it?

It is a _____

It is a

Find The Missing Vowel Sound

Find The Missing Vowel Sound

My Favorite Animals

lion fly monkey snake turtle bee crab

First, I like the
because
Then, I like the
because
Last, I like the
because

My favorite animals

snail
hippo
spider
bird
giraffe
dog
leopard

First, I like the
because
Then, I like the
because
Last, I like the
because

142

My Favorite Foods

 cassava

 groundpeas

 jollof rice

plantains

coconut

First, I like

because

Then, I like

because

Last, I like

because

144

Number Words

Spell the number 3 times.

Who are They?

| He / She / They | are / is a | grandma / mother / dad / babies / teachers |

Answer with full sentences.

She is a grandma.

_____

_____

146

Who are they?
Answer with full sentences.

Which Group Do They Belong In?
Trace the words then list them in the correct group.

lion truck car cat

train dog pig jet

bird fish boat bus

Vehicles

Animals

148

Which group do they belong in?

girl teacher man six

one three boy five

two baby four mom

People

Numbers

My Favorite Words

Read, Trace, and Write The Words

Read, trace, and
write the words.

I know my alphabet,

I know my spelling,

I know beginning sounds,

I know ending sounds,

and

I know punctuation.

I am an awesome reader.

We love reading.

Reading rocks!

Reading makes me smart.

Synonym Words

A synonym is a word that has the same or almost the same meaning as another word.

Trace and write the words.

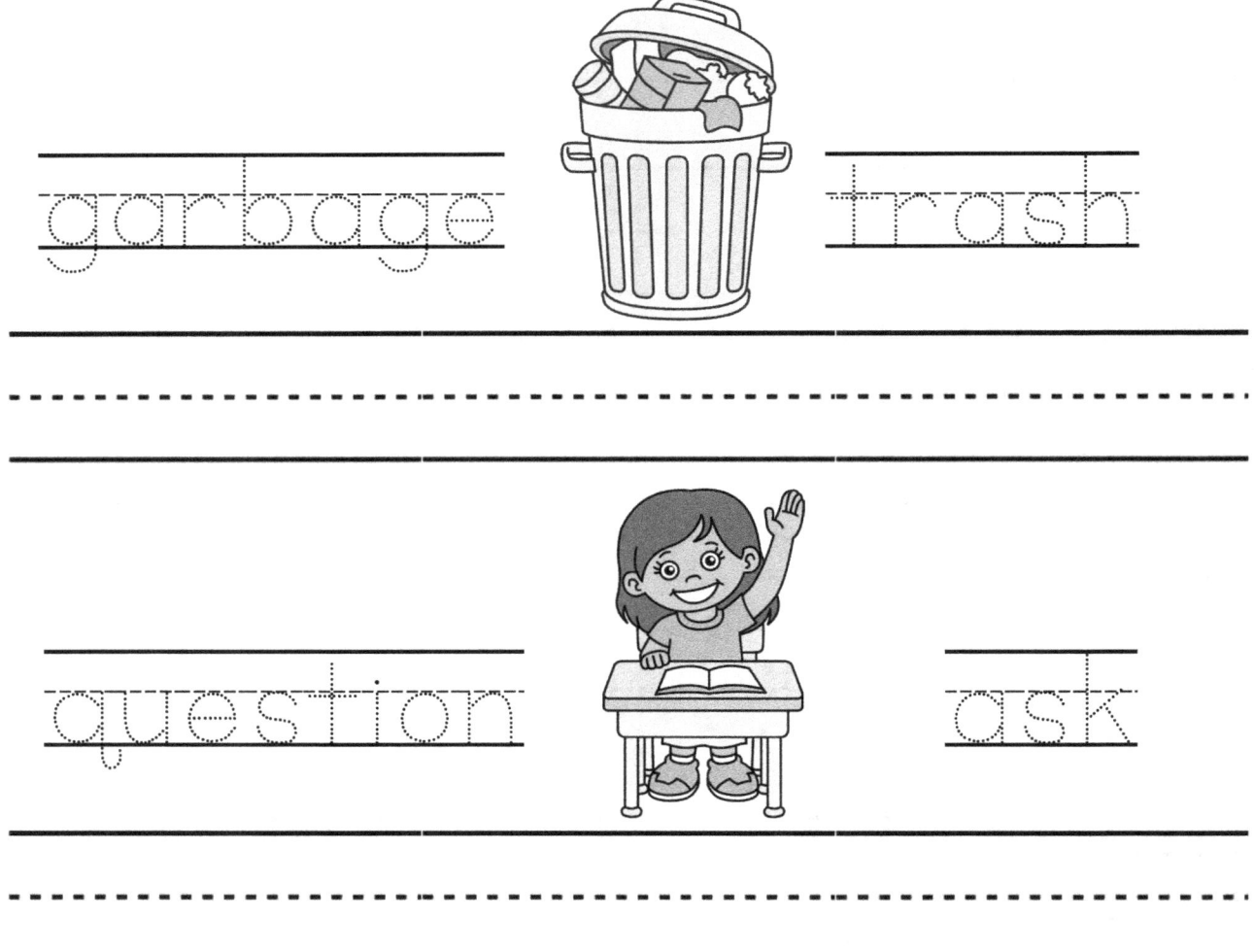

begin   start

large   big

cool   cold

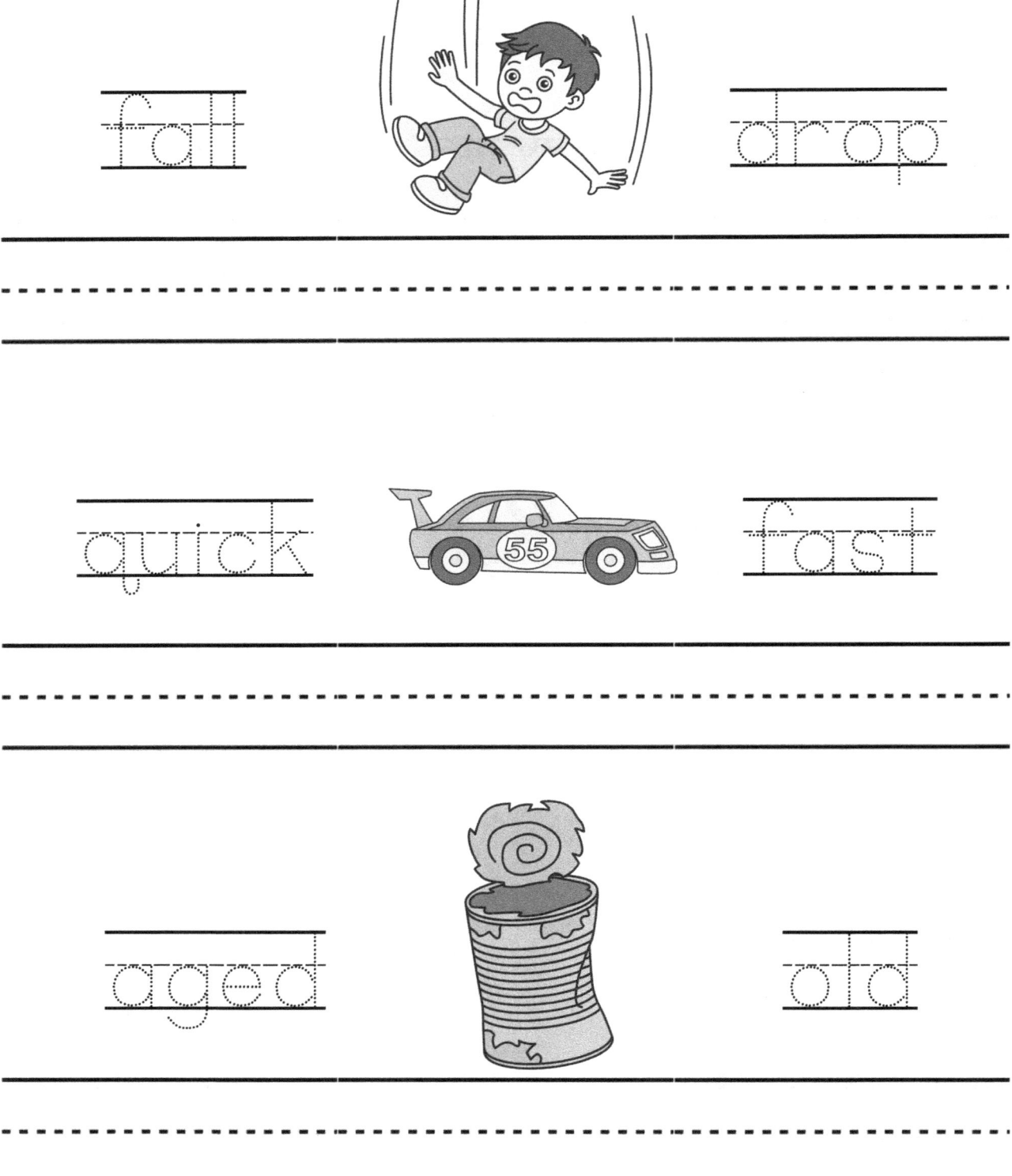

present  gift

cheerful  happy

finish  end

Compound Words

A compound word is a combination of two or more words that form one new word.

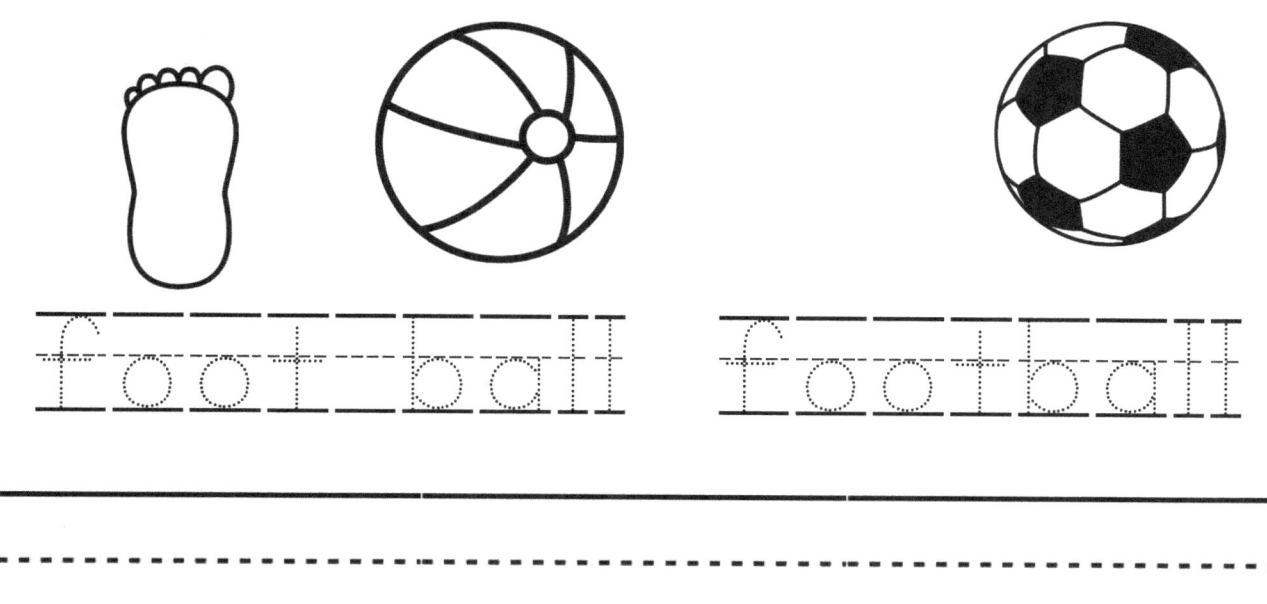

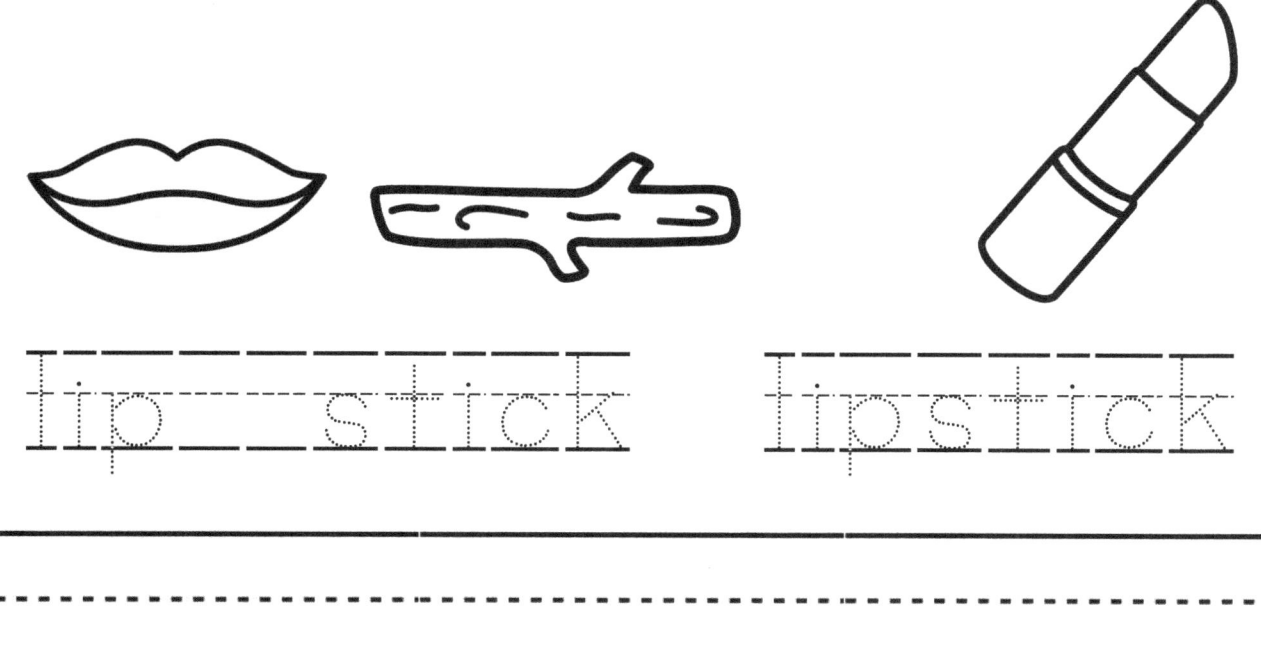

‾ ‾ ‾ ‾ ‾ ‾ ‾   ‾ ‾ ‾ ‾ ‾ ‾ ‾ ‾
pan   cake   pancake

‾ ‾ ‾ ‾ ‾ ‾ ‾ ‾ ‾ ‾
sunglasses

‾ ‾ ‾ ‾ ‾ ‾ ‾ ‾ ‾ ‾
sun glasses

Rhyming Words

Trace and write each rhyming word. They all end with 'ap' 'at' 'en' 'et' 'in' 'ip' 'it' 'op' 'ug' or 'ut'.

Rhyming Words

  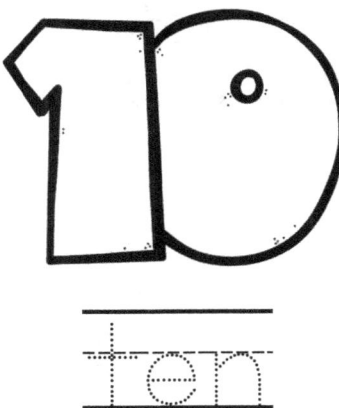

hen   ten

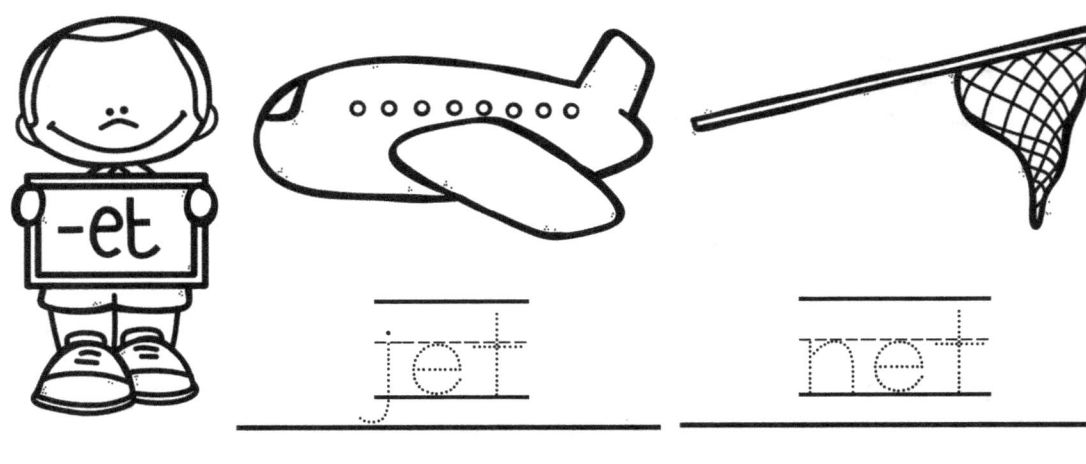

jet   net

wet

Write a rhyming word.

Read and Color

The ant is orange.

The goat is red.

The car is green.

The eggplant is purple.

The flea is brown.

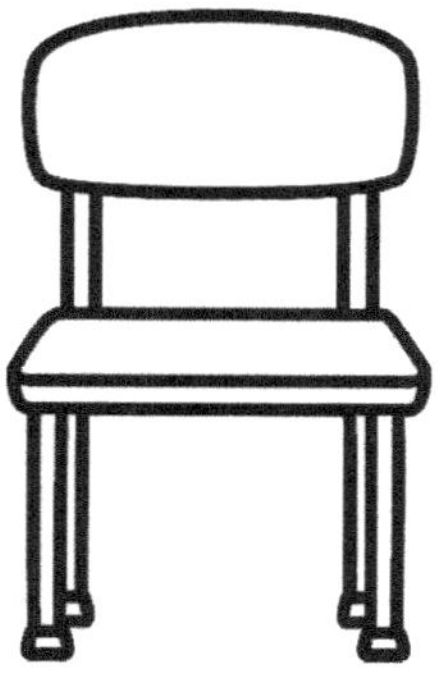

The pillow is blue.

The dress is pink.

The chair is brown.

The shirt is yellow.

Color the crayons.

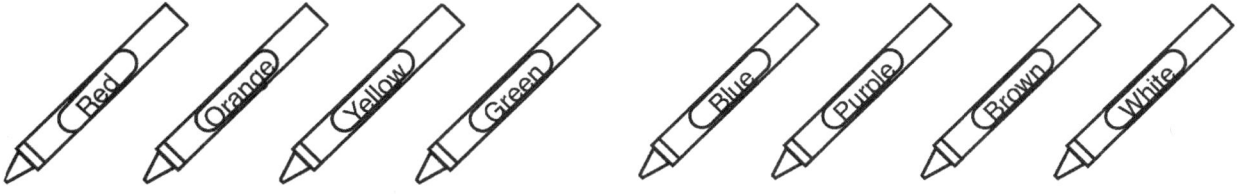

read   eat
pray   write

What Are They Doing?

She is praying.

He is reading.

He is writing.

She is eating.

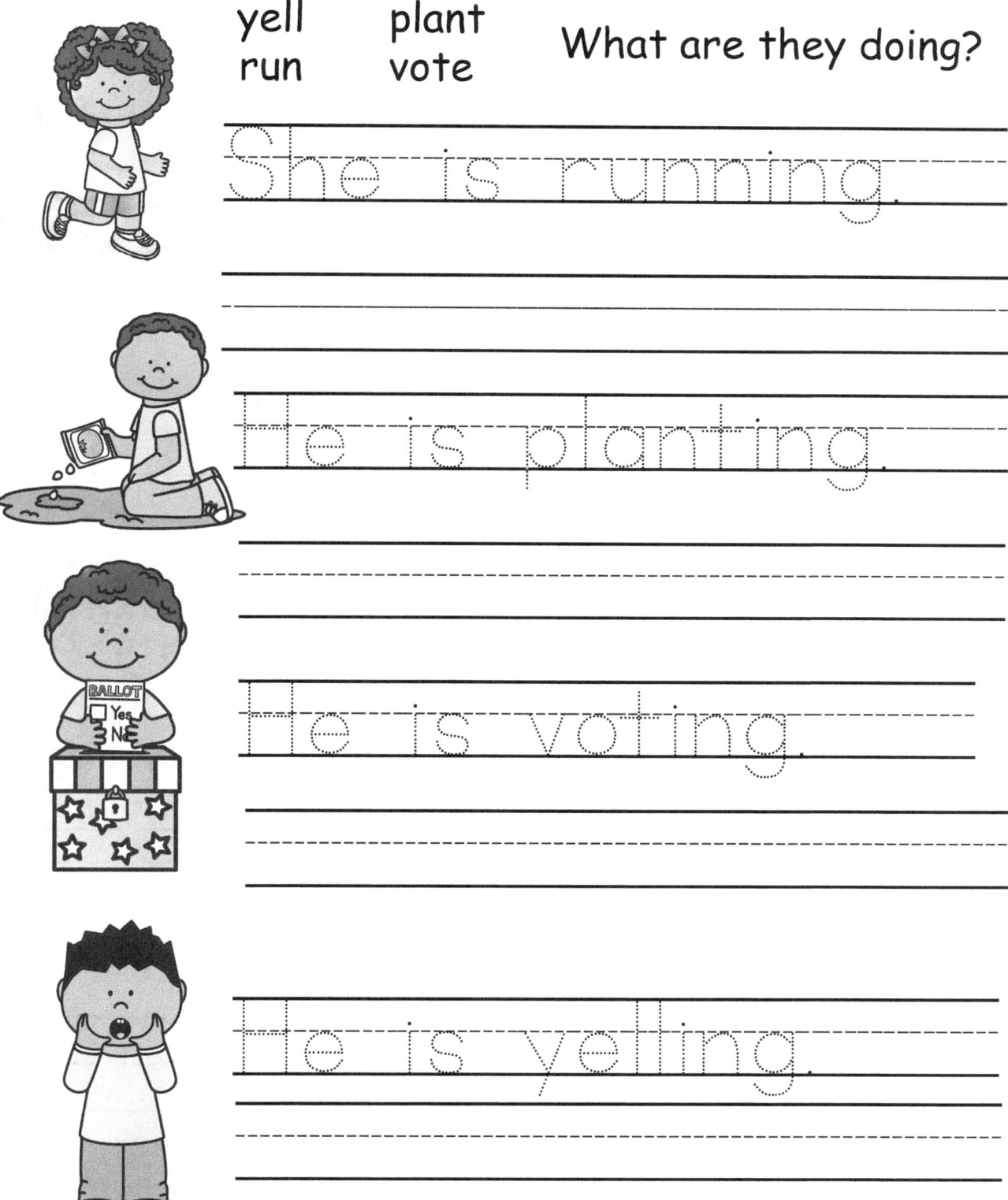

yell   plant
run   vote   What are they doing?

She is running.

He is planting.

He is voting.

He is yelling.

I Know Opposite Words

I can write some opposite words.

Bible Lessons

Genesis 1:1
In the
beginning,
God created
the heavens
and the Earth.

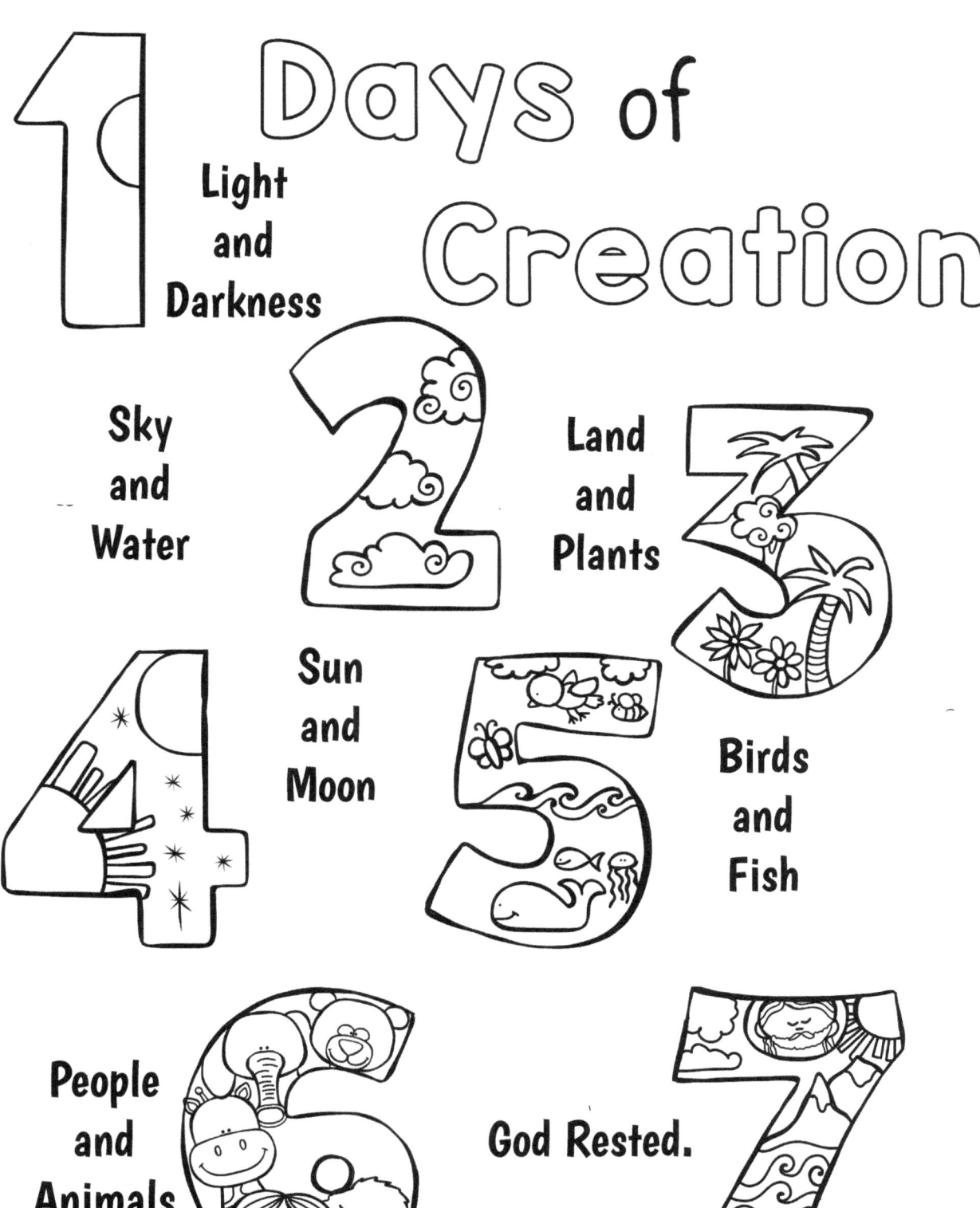

Light and Dark

Sky and Water

Land and Plant

Sun and Moon

Birds and Fish

People and

Animals

God rested

Noah's Ark

Fruit of the Spirit

Peace Kindness

Self-control

Faithfulness

Love Patience

Joy Gentelness

Goodness

Jesus loves me

Every word of
God proves true
Proverbs 30:5

GOD loves ME

Telling The Truth

Why is it important that we tell the truth? Are there some instances when lying is okay? Are we still being honest when we only tell part of the truth? Is it okay to leave something out when telling a story?

What does it mean to tell the truth?

Telling the truth is when you say what actually happened. If you don't tell the truth it's called telling a lie.

A lie is when you know the truth, but tell a different story.

I might not want to tell the truth, because I am scared and I could get in trouble.

Lying will get me in more trouble than telling the truth.

Telling the truth is always the right thing to do.

Honesty

I will tell the truth.

Alway tell the truth.

Honesty

Honesty means telling the truth. Telling the truth can be hard, especially when you've done something wrong. But when you tell the truth, you show people you respect and care about them. When you tell a lie, it makes your mistakes even bigger. The opposite of honesty is dishonesty. Dishonesty makes people feel bad. It makes you feel bad too. When you are honest, you can make your mistakes better. You can fix things and get back to having fun. You can be brave and tell the truth. You can say, "I made a mistake, but I'm going to be honest about it." Being honest is hard, but it is an important part of being a good student, family member, and friend. Honesty helps your friends and family, but it helps you, too. You feel better when you tell the truth.

When we are sharing our ideas and experiences, it is best to be honest and truthful about what we are saying. But sometimes when it is time to share our experiences, instead of being honest and truthful, we make up a story that is not true. It is because we want to impress our friends, or to make us seem more interesting. Other times, we might be dishonest or make up a story if we want to keep from getting in trouble. We might be dishonest or make up a story if we want to get someone else in trouble. We might be dishonest or make up a story if we are trying to keep a friend out of trouble. We might be dishonest or make up a story if we are using our imagination about what we wished would have happened. We might be dishonest or make up a story if we are embarrassed about something we have done. Being dishonest or making up a story instead of telling the truth when we are sharing ideas and experiences is not a good choice to make. Being dishonest causes the people around us to lose some trust in us. They start to worry that we will not be truthful in other situations too. Sometimes when we make up one story, we have to keep making up more stories to cover up the first untrue story we told. Being dishonest can also cause someone else to get in trouble even when that person may not have done anything wrong.

Our stories explain who we are. Everyone is different and everyone has a different story to tell. When we make up stories, those stories don't belong to just us, they belong to others too. Your classmates and your teacher will be proud of you if you are honest and tell true stories. You will be proud of yourself too.

Practical — Memorize The Promise and recite it every day.

The Promise
Being myself and telling the truth is a better choice to make. It is important to love myself, and to be proud of myself. I don't need to make up stories or be dishonest about what I have done.

Taking Others' Things
"Finders" does not mean "Keepers". You shouldn't take things that don't belong to you.

Building Trust
What does it mean to trust someone? Trust means that someone will always be there for you and help you when they can. You know they will be there. How do you build trust? You look at someone when you talk to them, and do what you say you are going to do.

Friendship

Friendship is a warm and kind feeling or attatude toward someone.
I can be a friend.

I am a good friend.

I give and share.

I tell the truth.

Positive vs. Negative Behavior

Behavior means the way in which a person acts. We all act in a particular way by what we choose to do. It is good to think carefully before you decide what to do. That way, you select the Good Choice and not the Bad Choice.

Good Choice = Positive Behavior

Listening to the teacher.
Focusing on my work.
Staying on task.
Staying in my seat.
Raising my hand.

Always tell the truth.

Working together. Giving a high-five.
Cleaning up. Helping a friend.
Being a good friend.

Not giving up. If at first you don't succeed, try. . . try. . . again.

Being appreciative.
Listening and thinking.
Staying quiet in line.
Being responsible.
Using self-control.

Bad Choice = Negative Behavior

Bad Choices – Not working as a team. Not telling the truth. Not listening. Pushing & throwing things. Using unkind words.

Drawing/scribbling on someone's paper. Copying someone else's work. Making a mess. Ripping paper. Distracting others.

Making a mess.

Invading a person's space. Kicking objects or kicking someone. Teasing. Pushing someone. Stealing from someone.

Behavior Sort

Sort out the behavior by the pictures. Mark G next to the picture for good behavior, and B next to the picture for bad behavior.

Not working as a team.

Caring.

Pushing & throwing things.

Being kind.

Kicking things.

Working as hard as you can.

Being neat.

Telling a lie.

Stealing someone's candy.

Rude, Mean, & Bad
Be a Buddy, NOT a Bully
Are you a good friend?
Do you use kind and caring words when talking with others?

Away With Bullying!

Color the balloons with the kind and caring words.

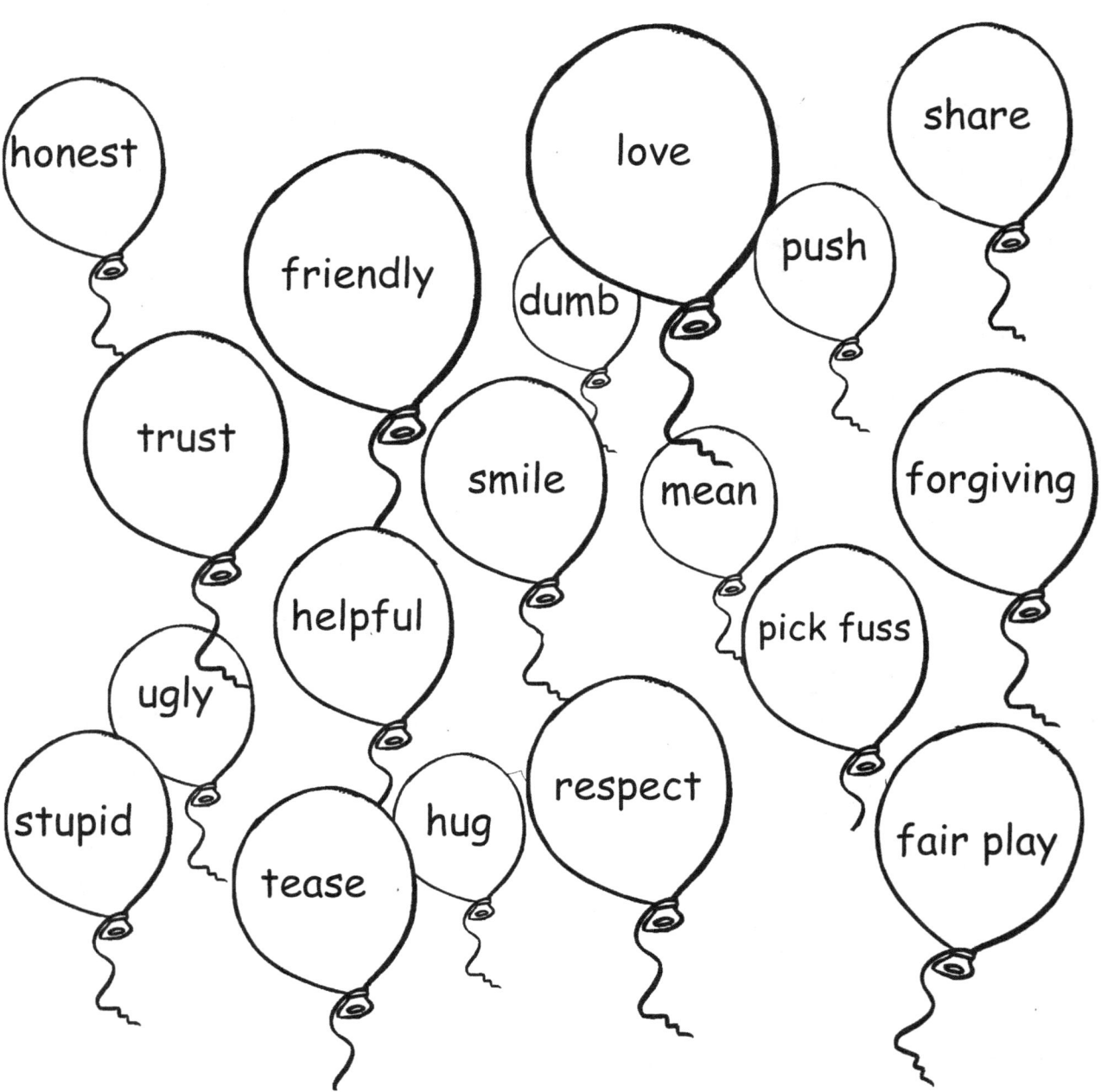

Kind and Caring Words

Sad, Mad, or Glad

When something happends, it's ok for us to be sad, or mad, or glad.
It's ok for us to be scared too. Our emotion is like a light bulb.

When we feel happy and confident, our light shines BRIGHT!

When we feel sad, angry, or upset, our light might be DIM (less bright).

When your light feels dim, there are things you can do to brighten it! Some of these ideas might help you COPE and some of them might bring you COMFORT.

Cry.
Draw a picture.
Hug someone.
Talk to someone that you trust.
Hug a pillow.
Write about how you feel.
Do something that you really enjoy.
Count your breaths.

When I am sad, I will . . .

Table Manners

table manners

I mind my table manners.

I make sure my hands are clean before eating.
I sit still in my chair during mealtime.
I take small bites of my food and keep my mouth closed while chewing.
Smacking or slurping my food or drink is rude.
I chew my food before I talk.
I use a napkin when I have food on my face.
I ask to be excused if I want to leave the table.

My Best Art   Draw a picture.

Date: _____

Draw a picture.

Date: _____

Draw a picture.

Date: _____

Draw a picture.

Date: _____

Draw a picture.

Date: _____

Draw a picture.

Date: _____